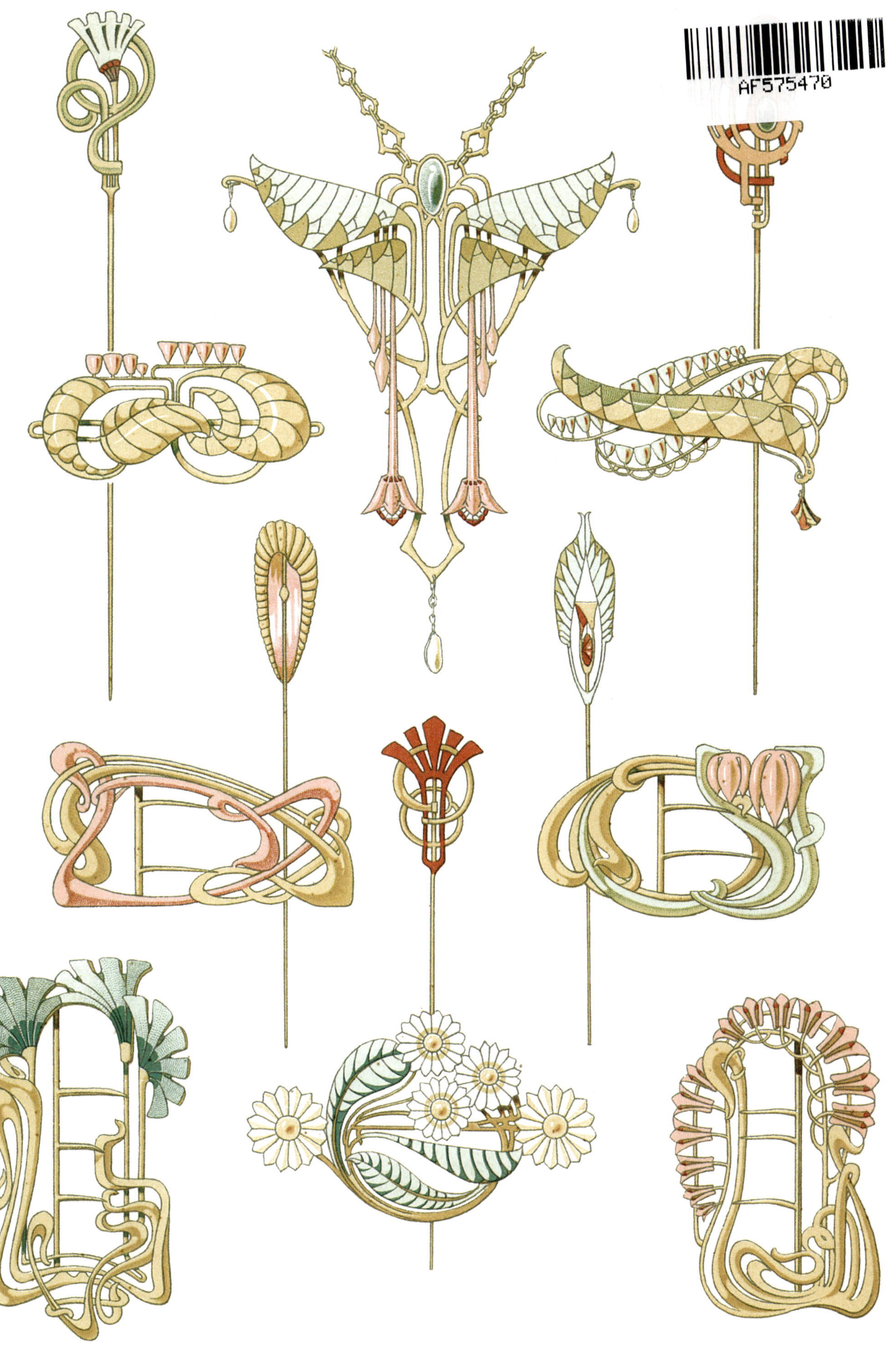

Designed by R. Beauclair

PLATE 1

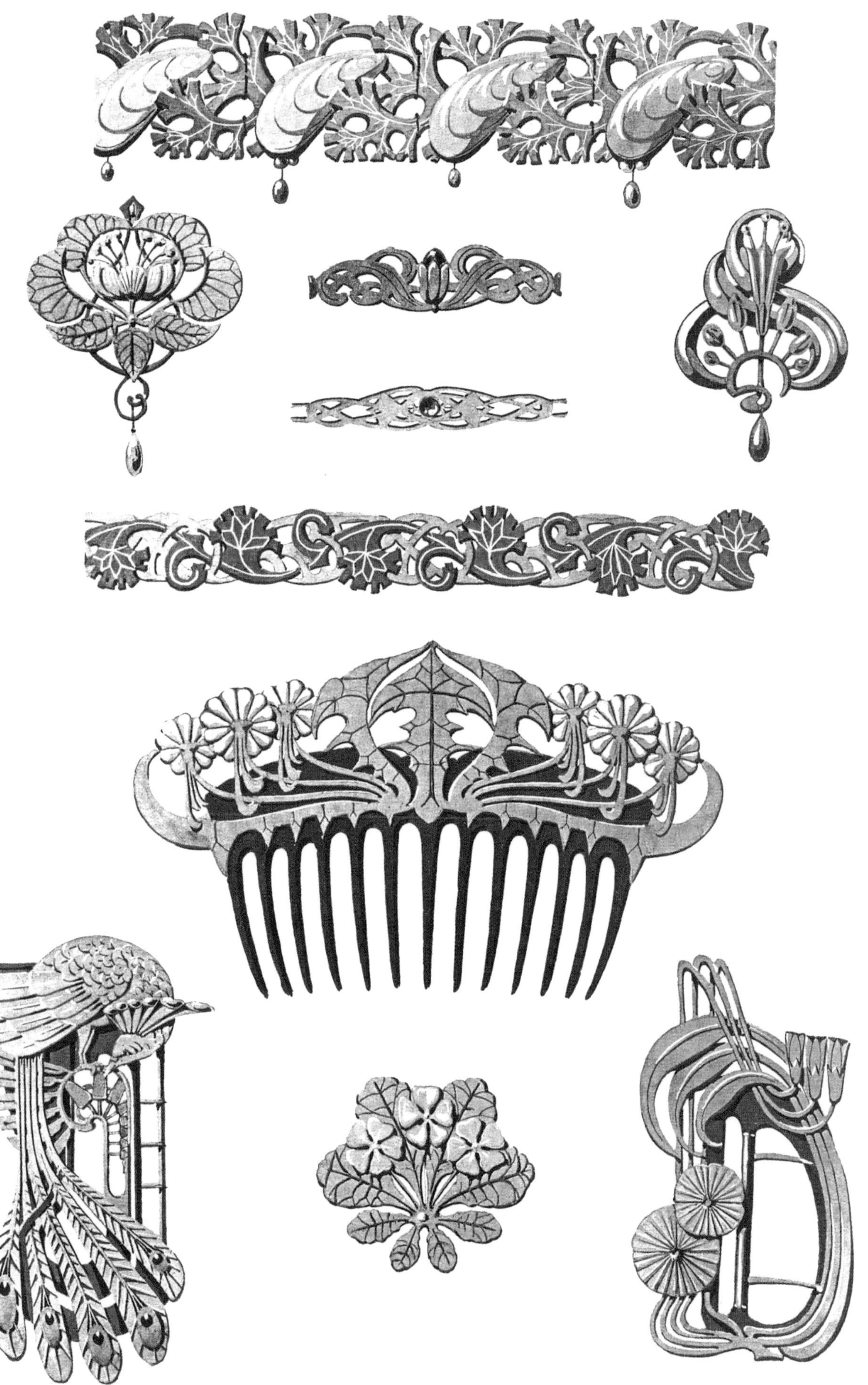

Designed by A. Petitjean

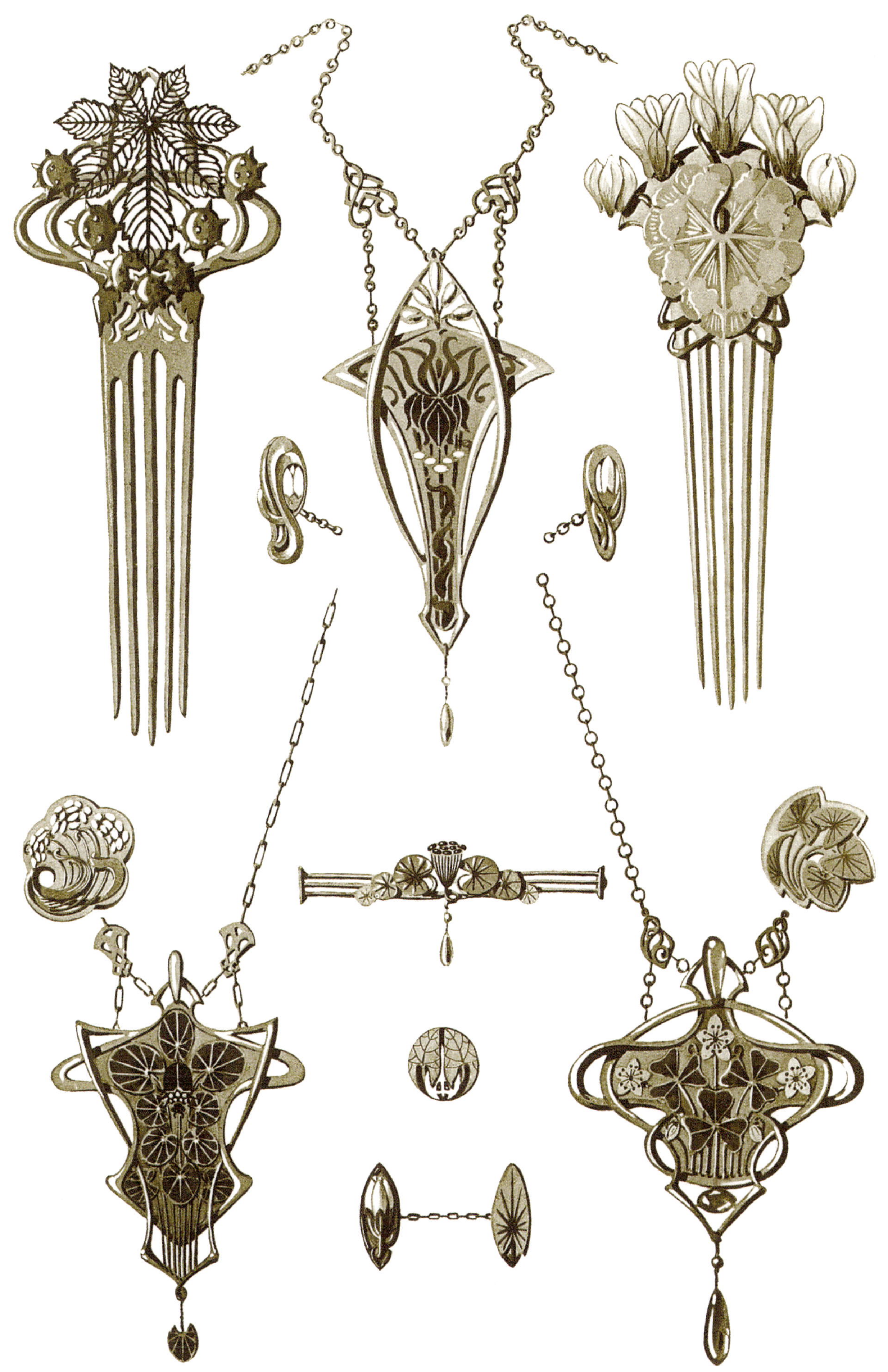

Designed by Paul Liénard

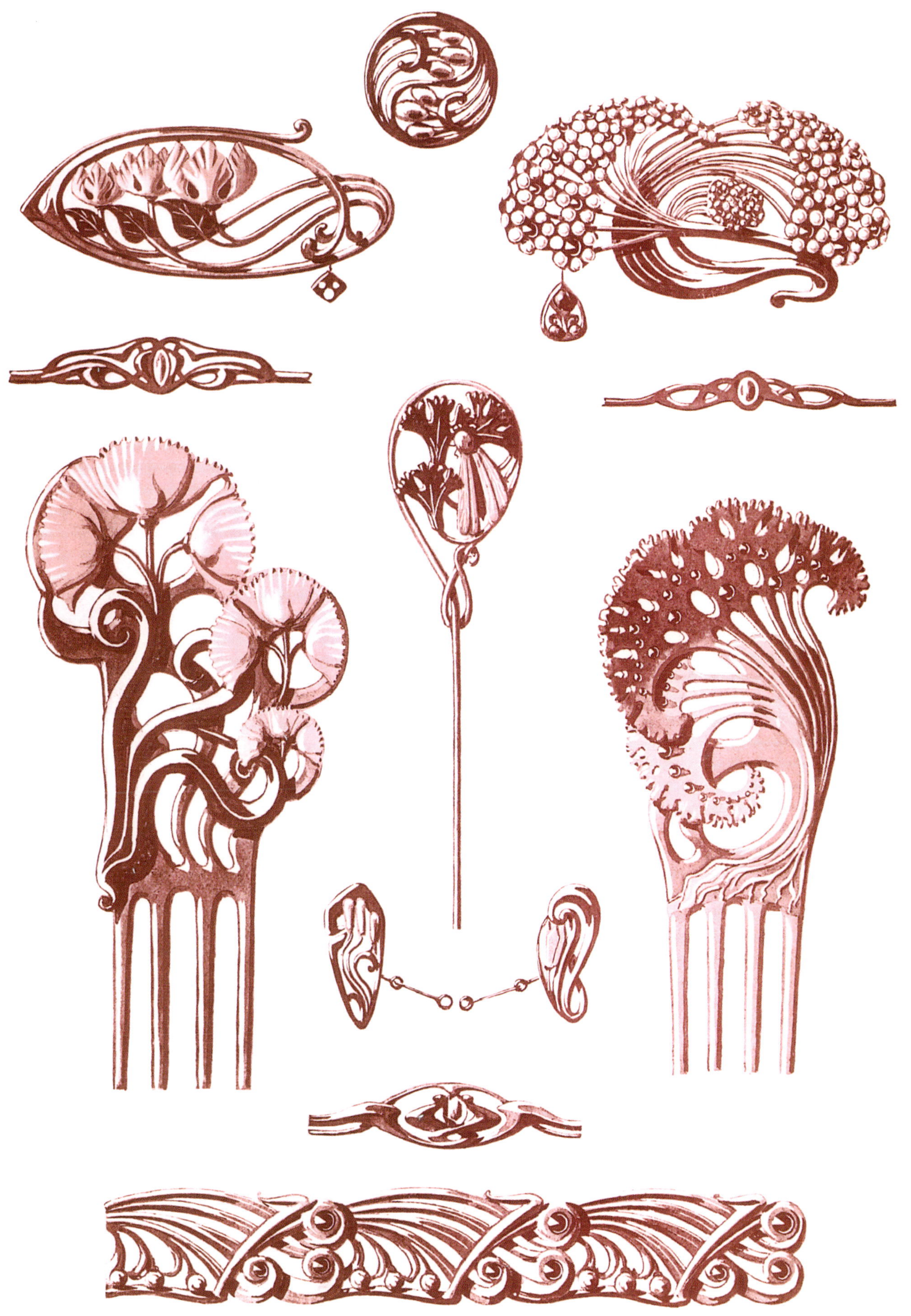

Designed by P. F. Follot

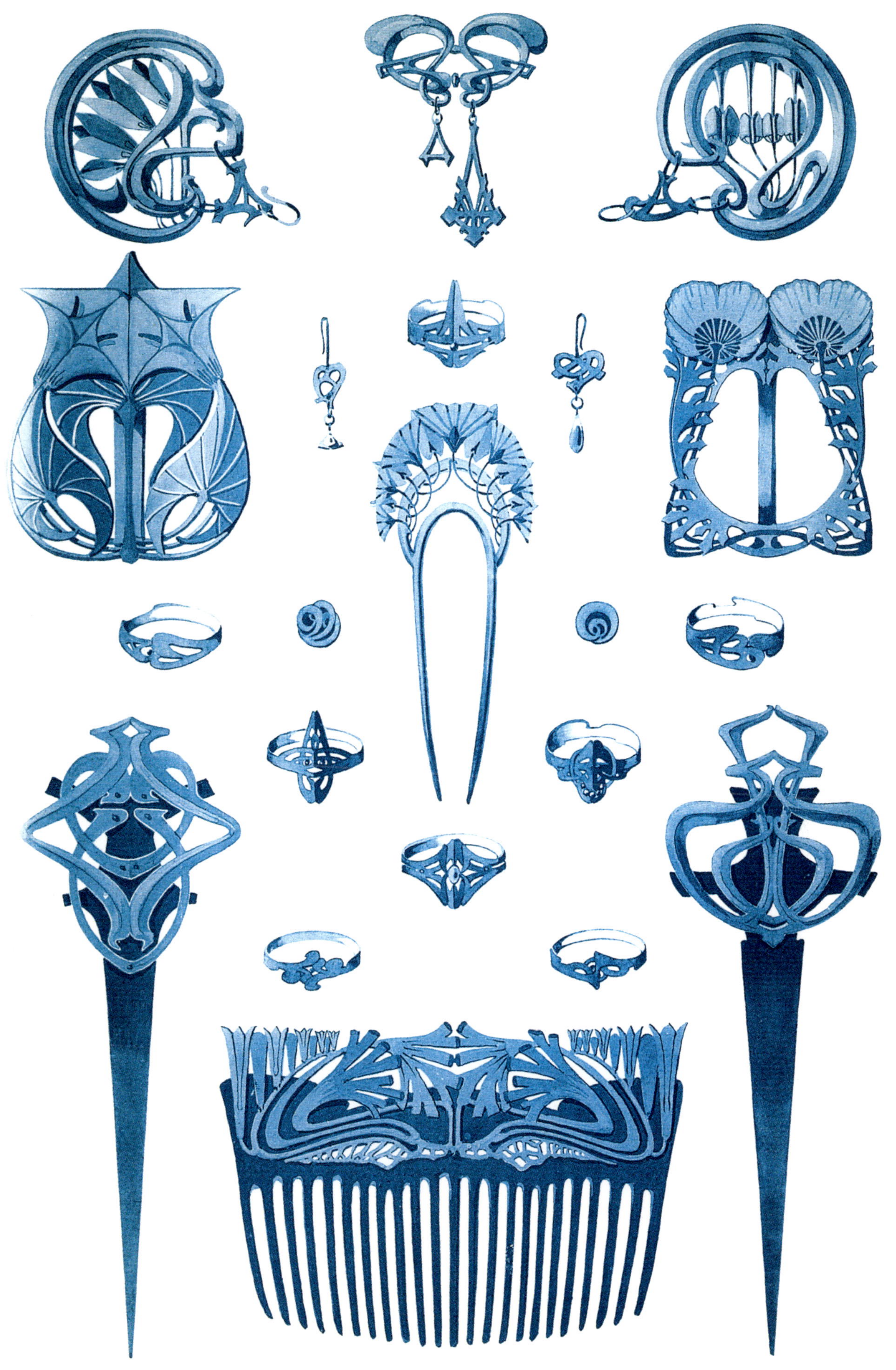

Designed by R. Beauclair

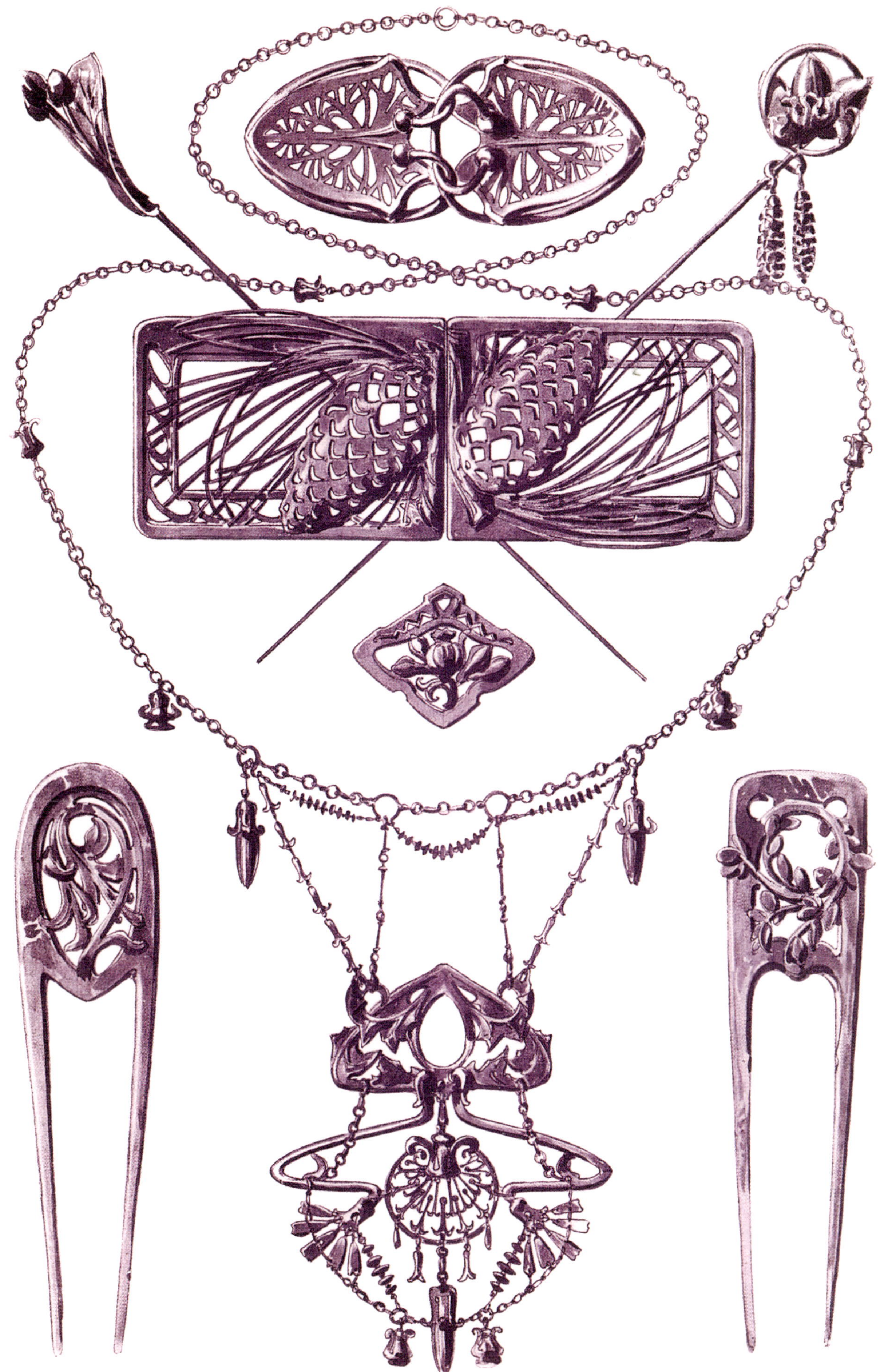

Designed by J. Armbruster

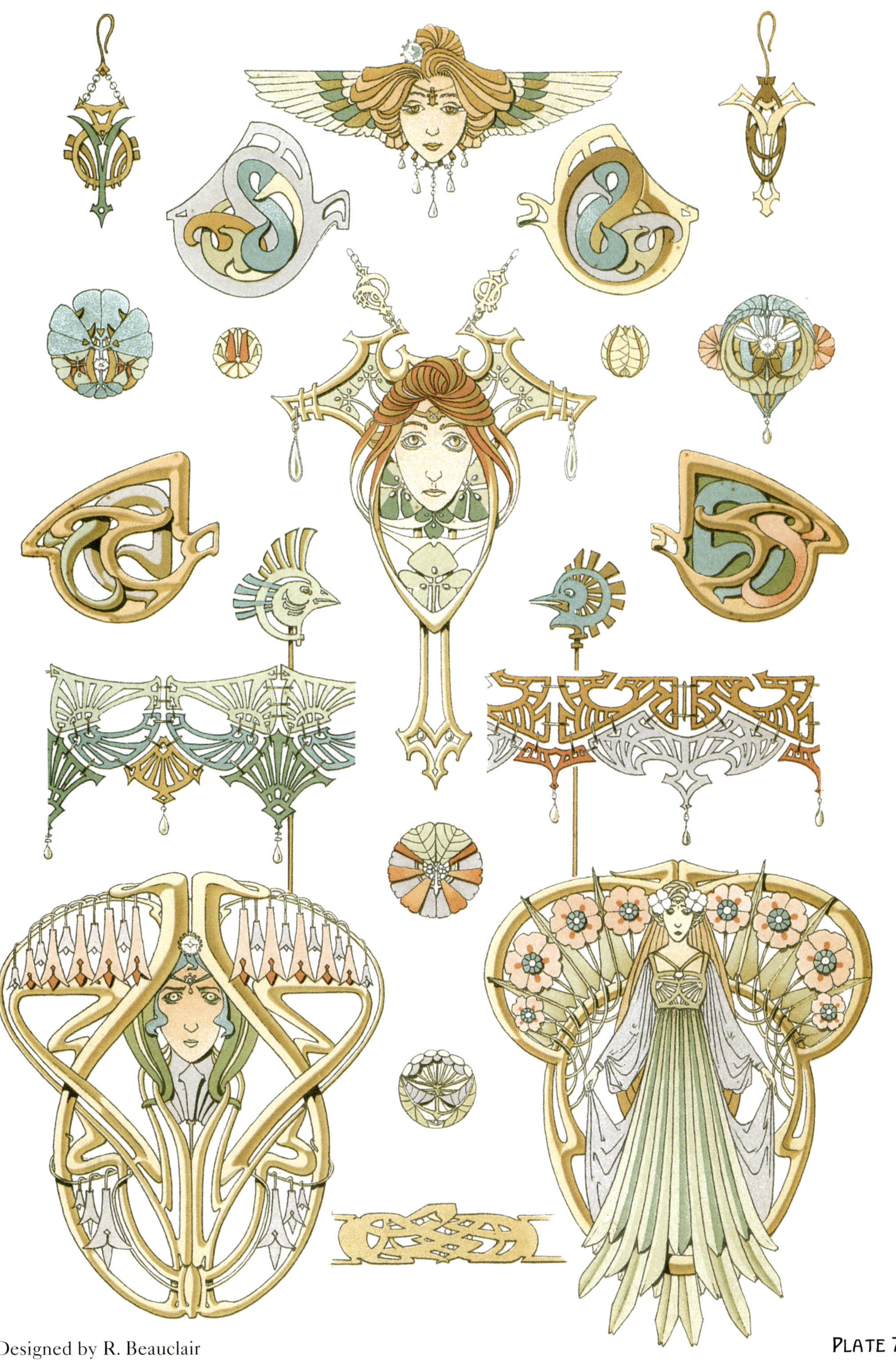

Designed by R. Beauclair

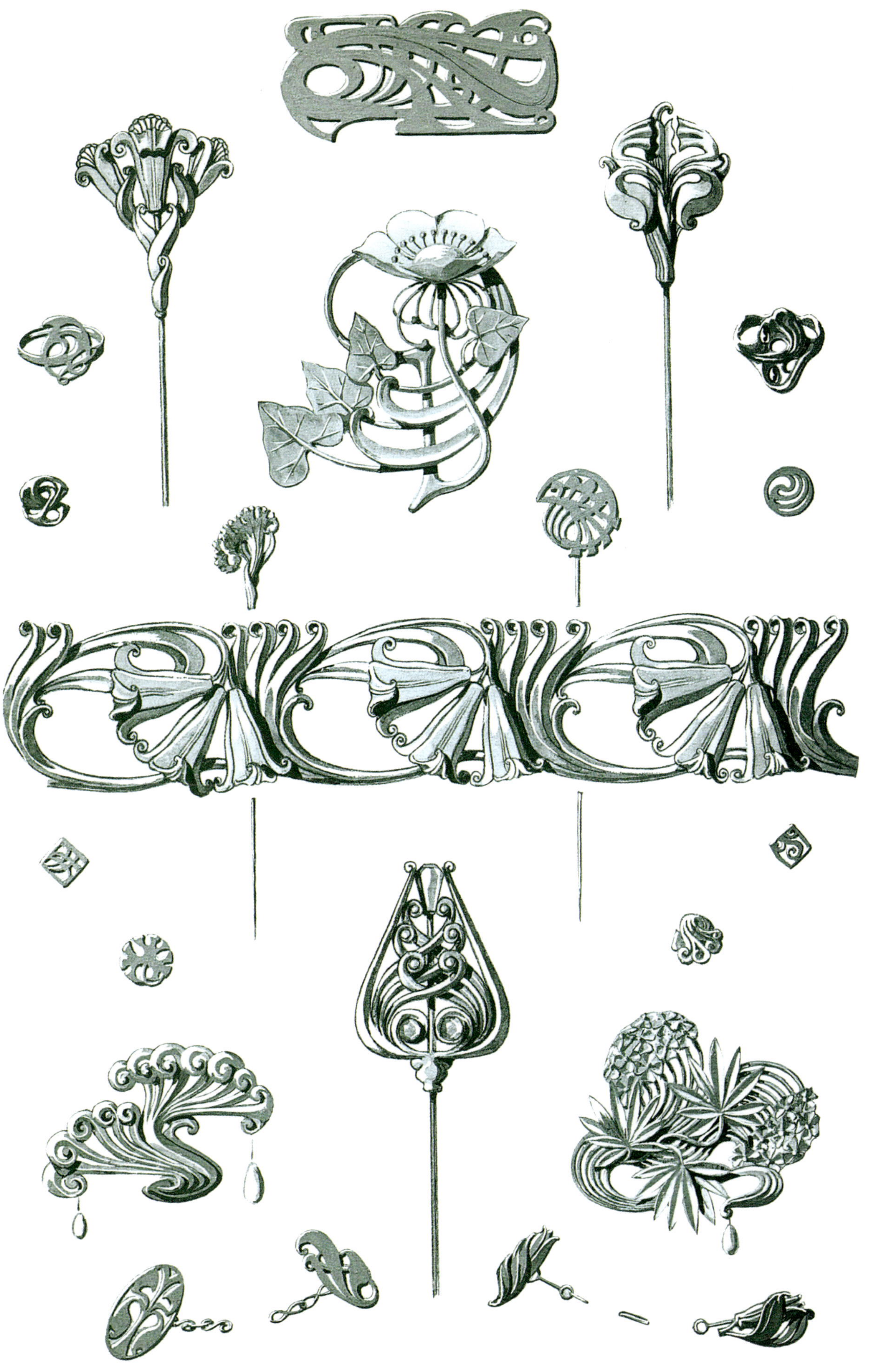

Designed by P. F. Follot

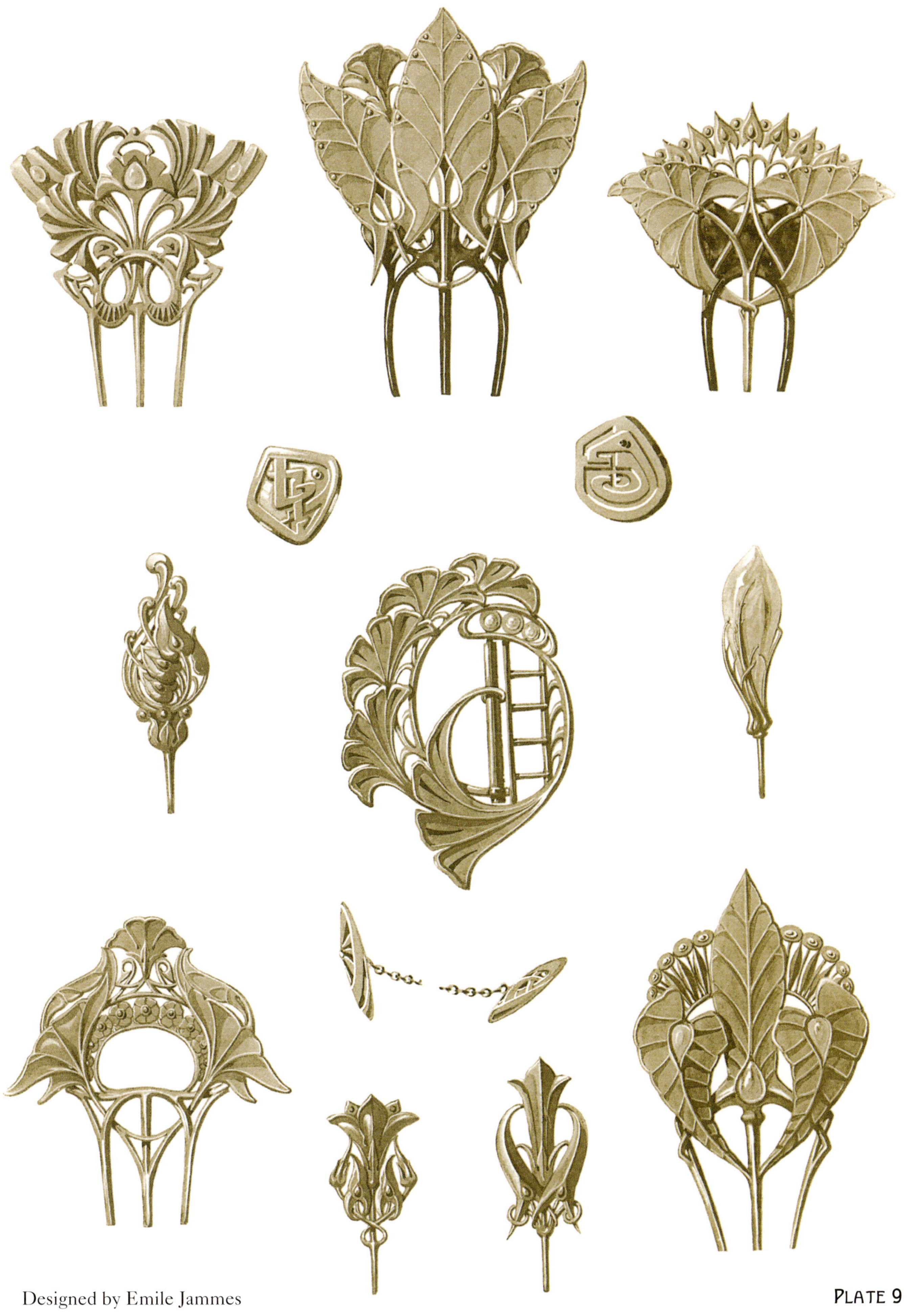

Designed by Emile Jammes

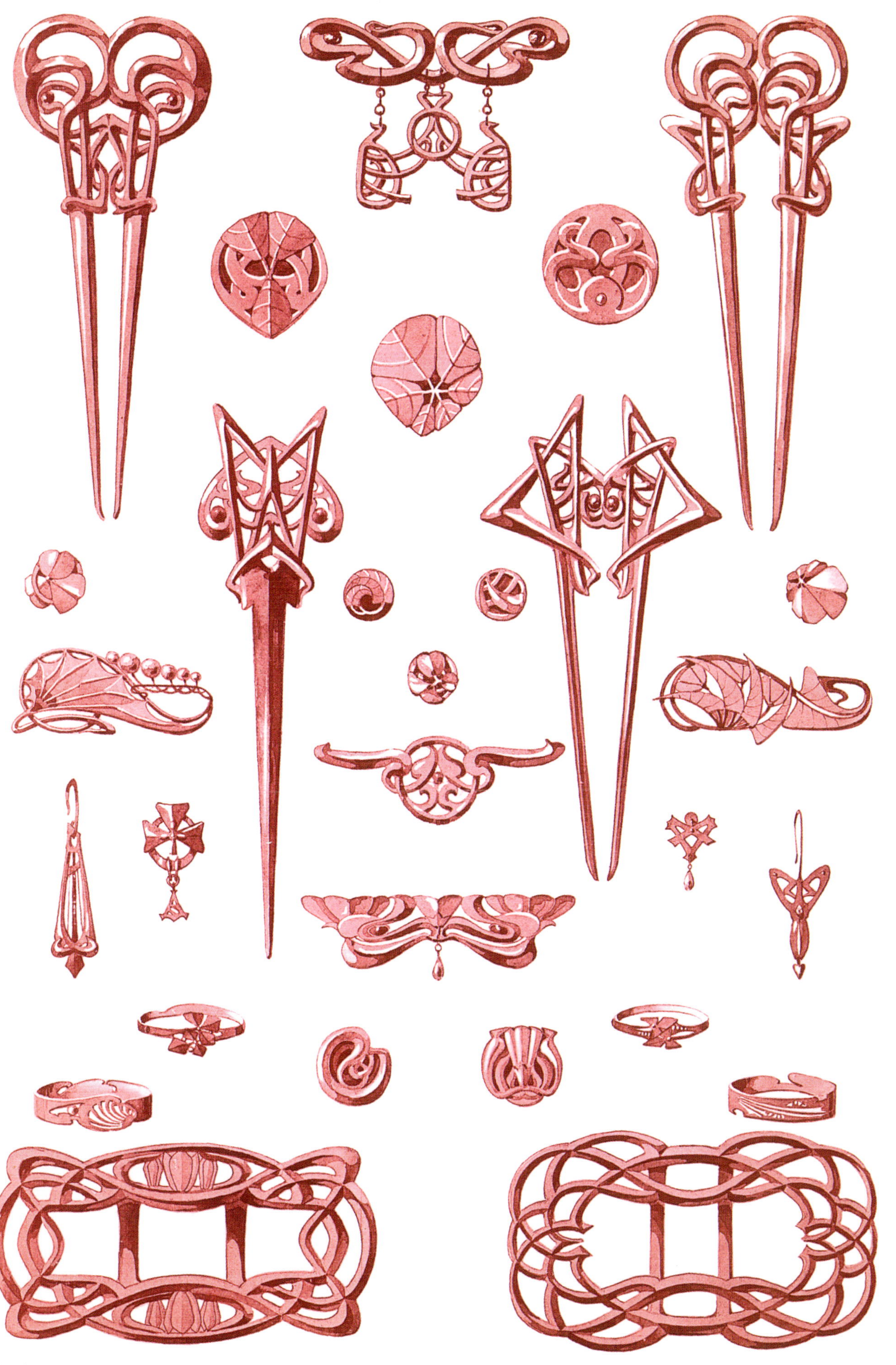

Designed by R. Beauclair

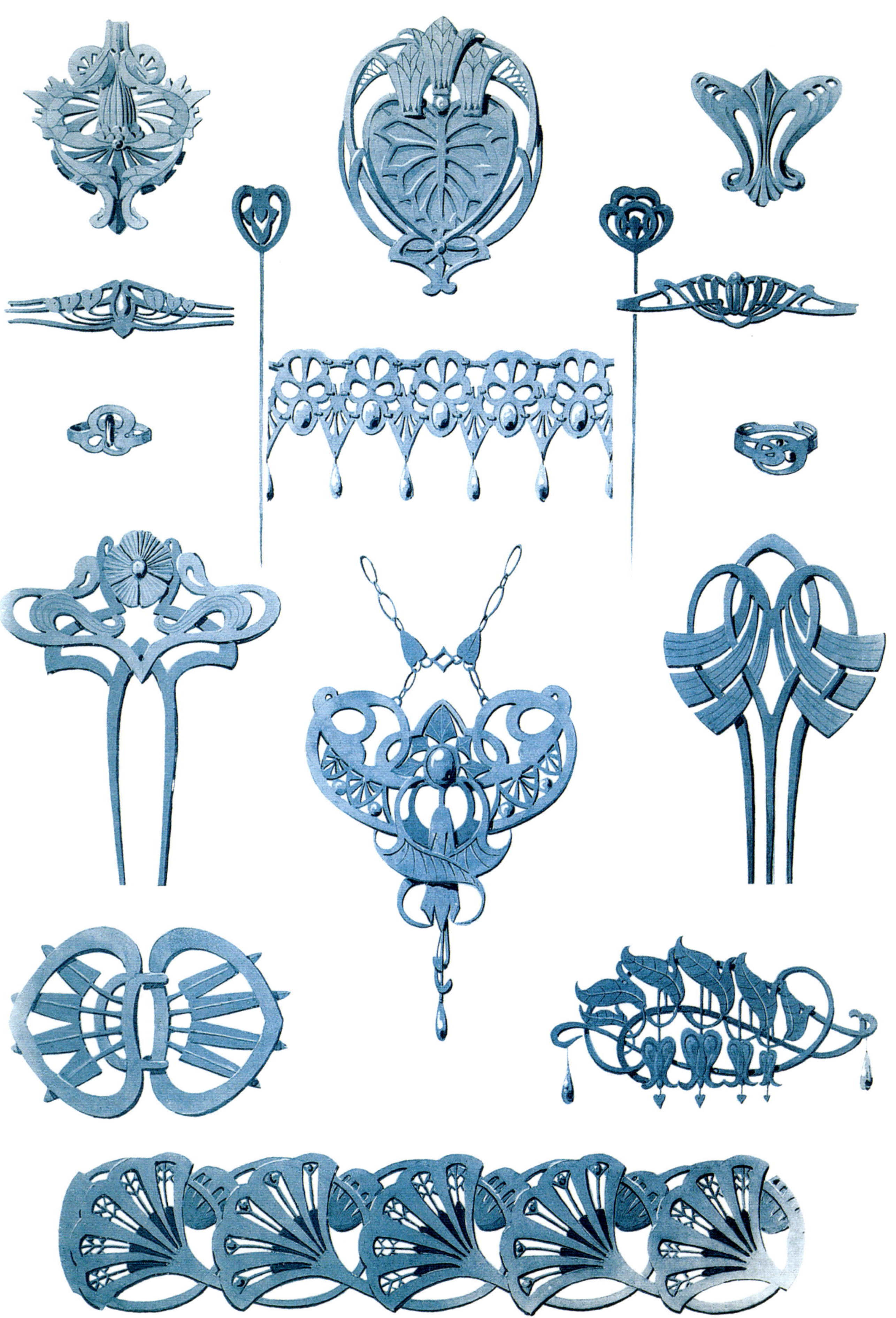

Designed by A. Petitjean

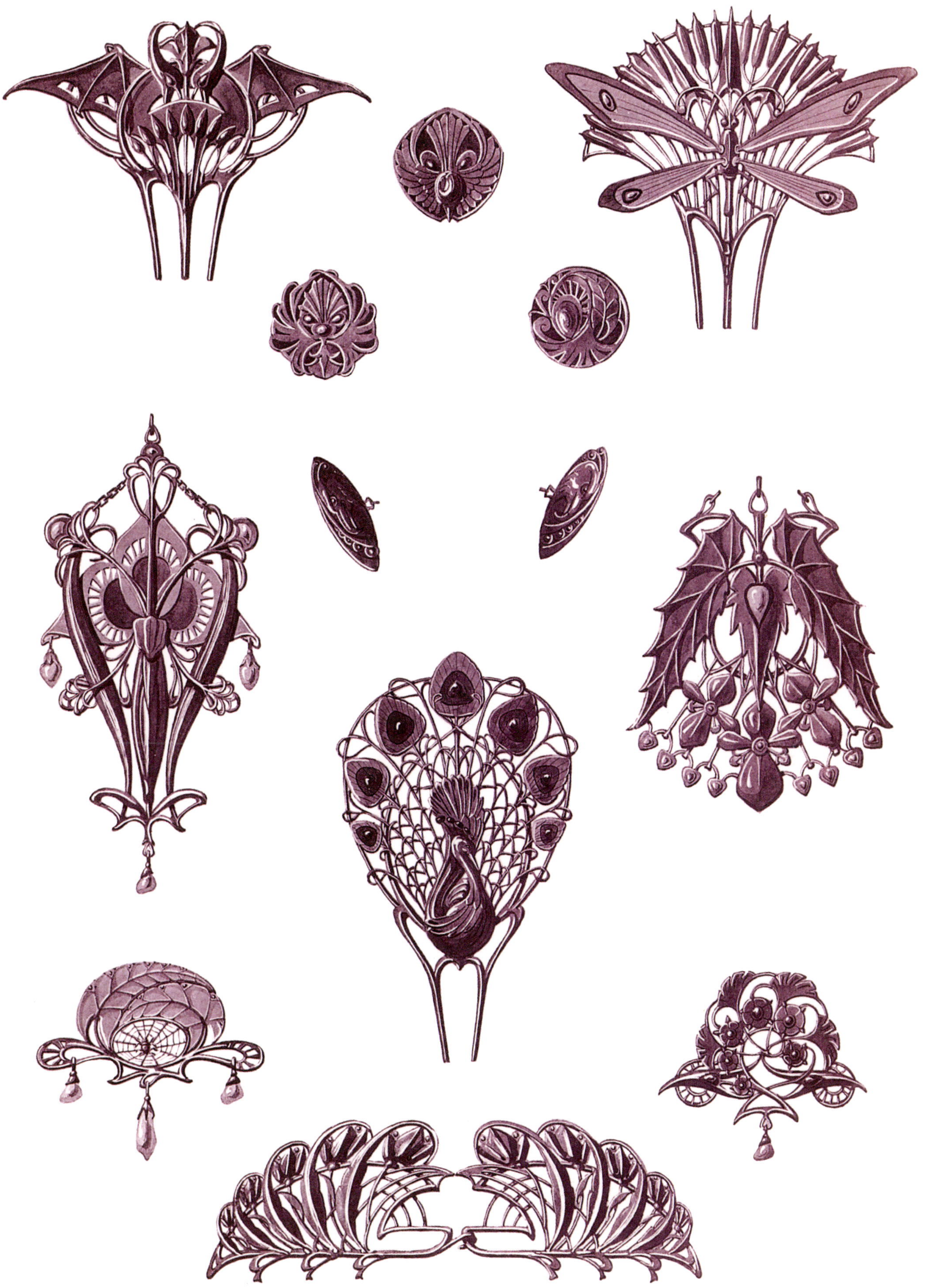

Designed by Emile Jammes

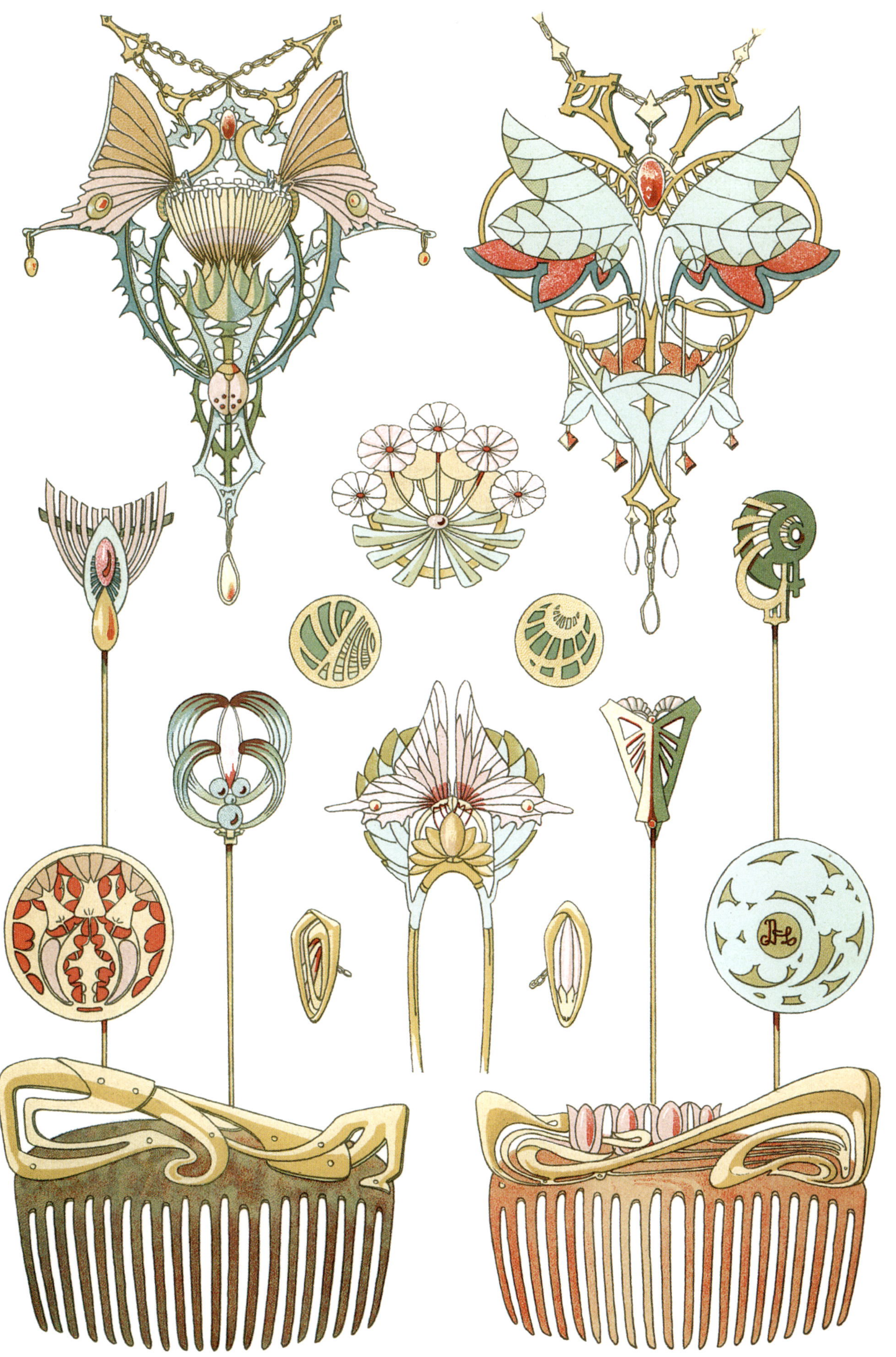

Designed by R. Beauclair

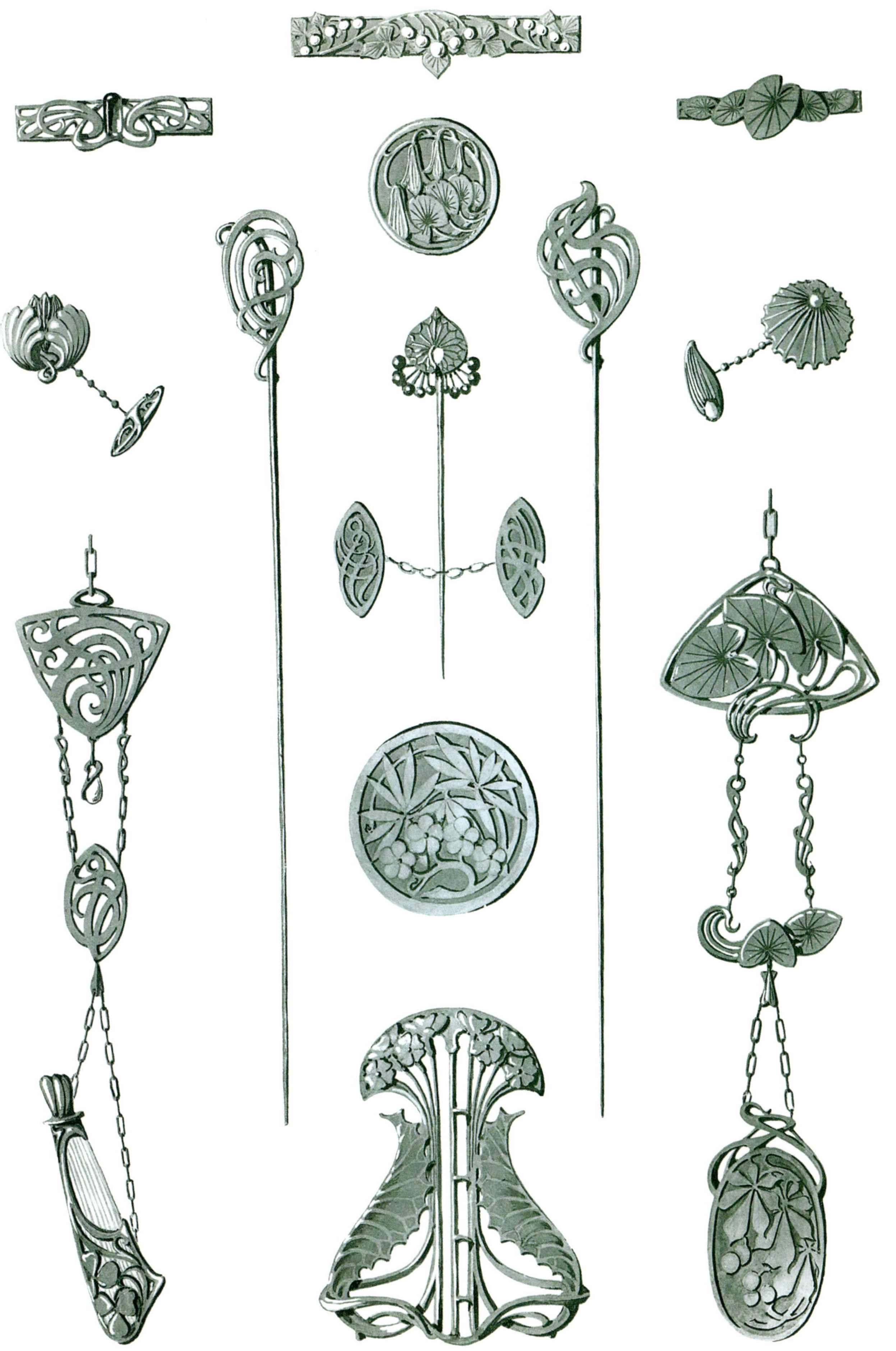

Designed by Paul Liénard

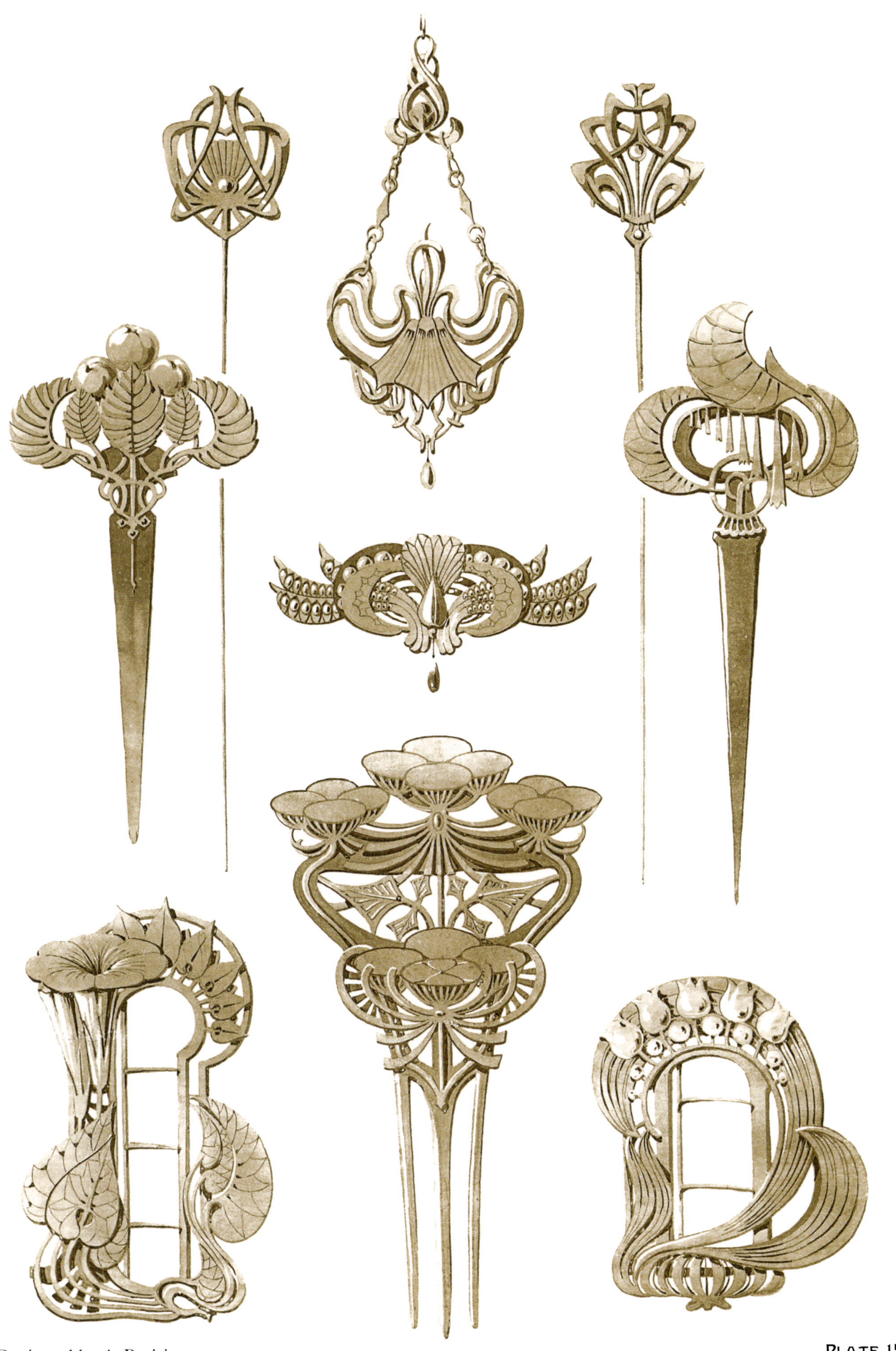

Designed by A. Petitjean

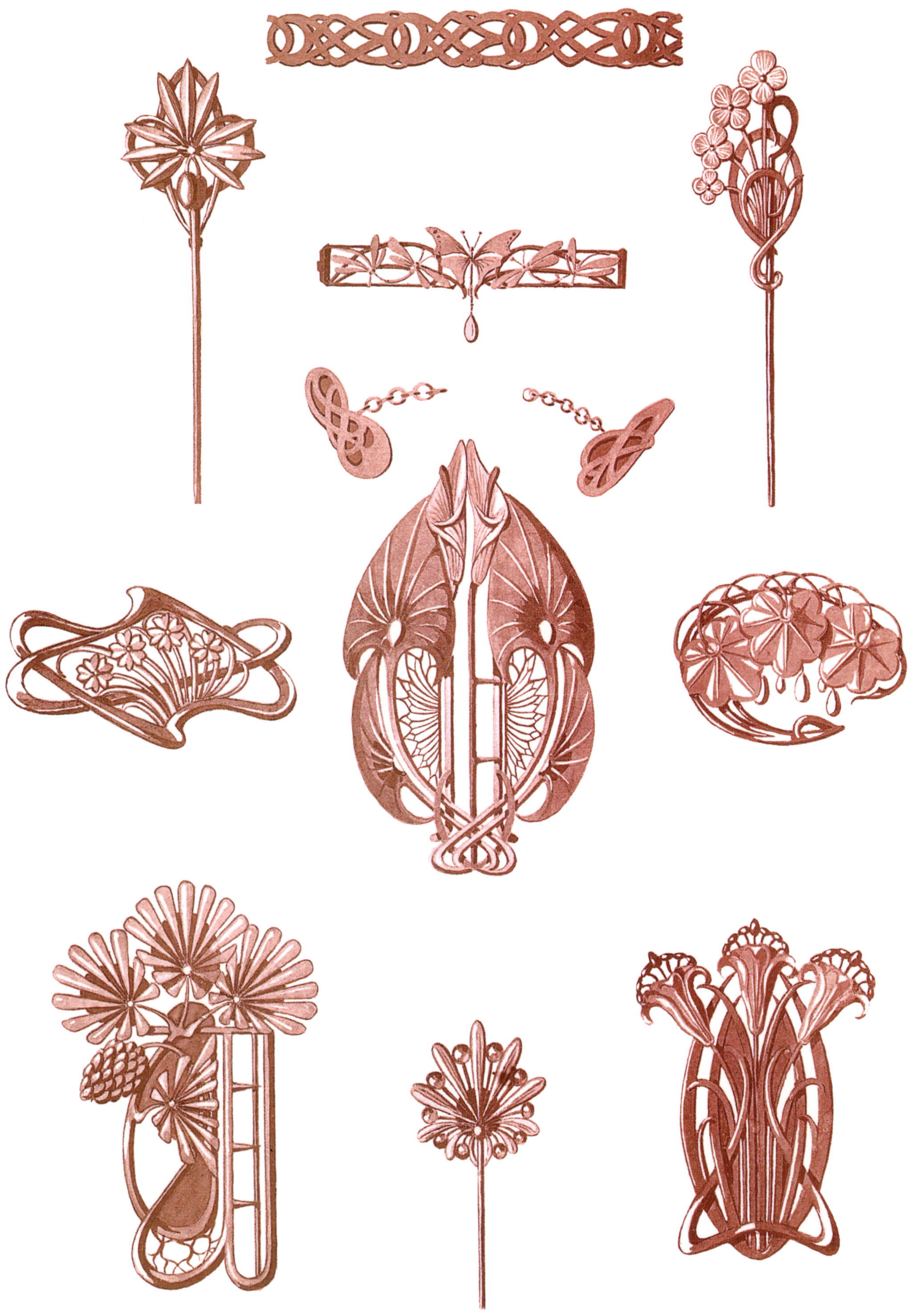

Designed by Paul Liénard

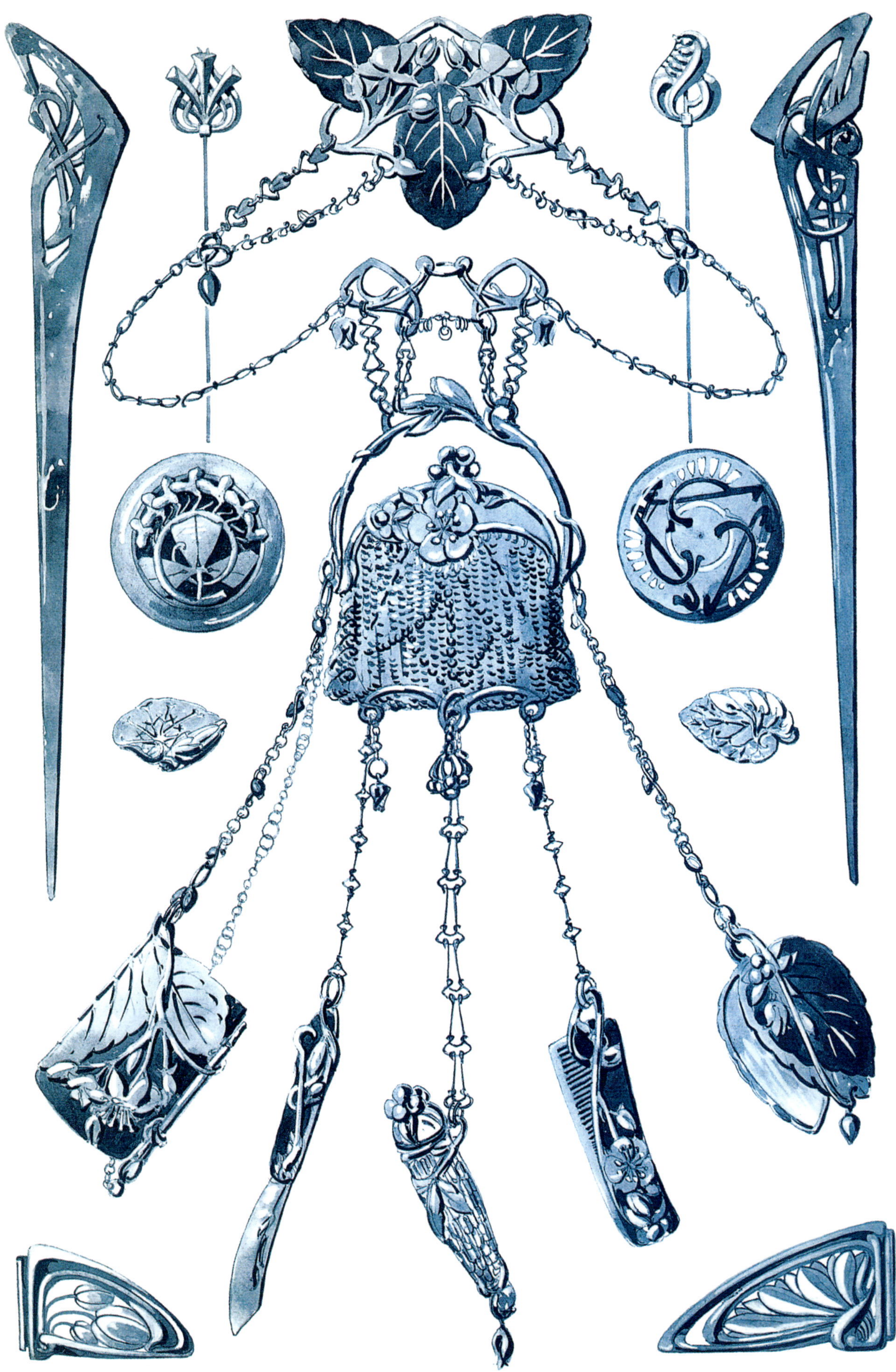

Designed by J. Armbruster

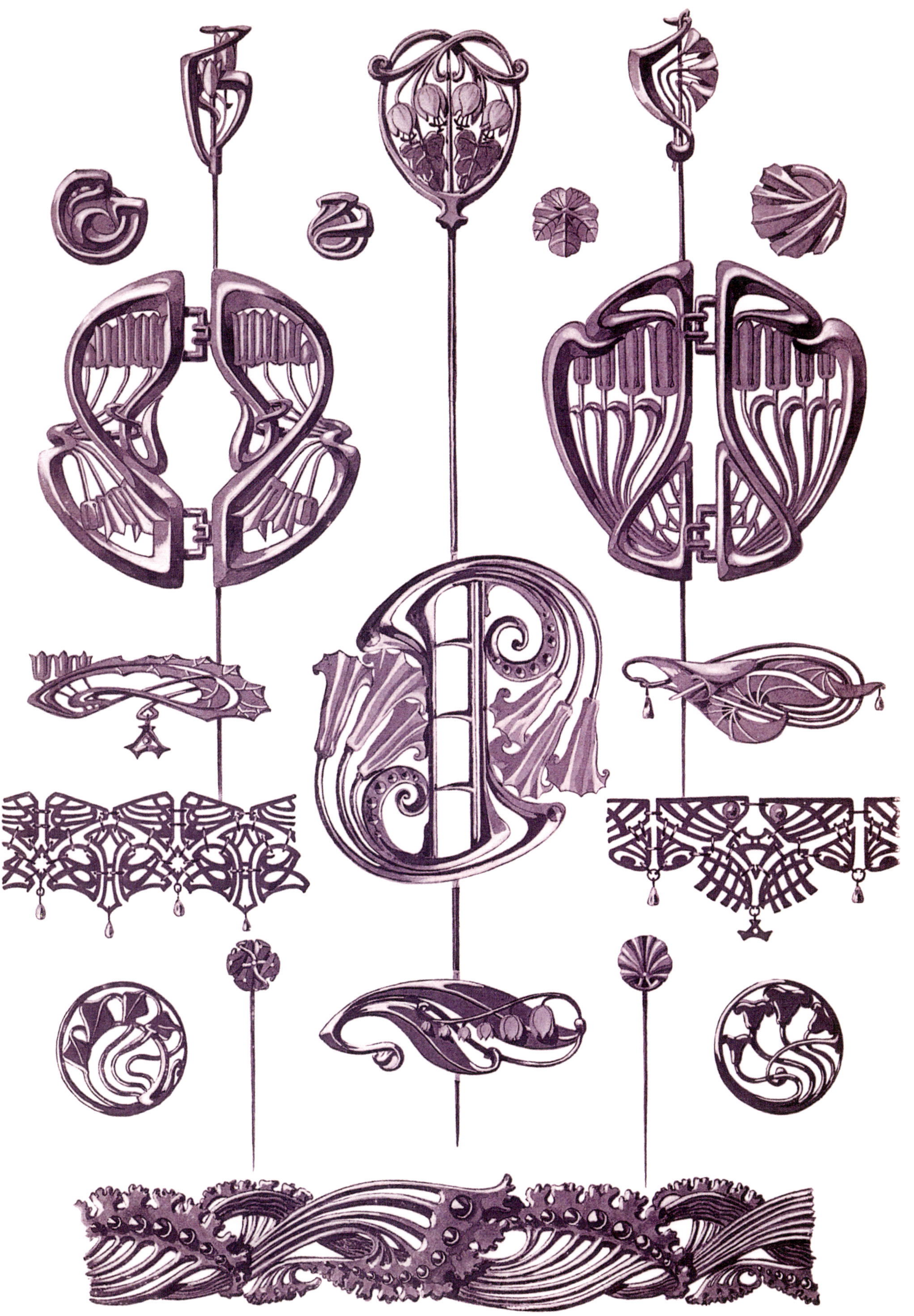

Designed by R. Beauclair

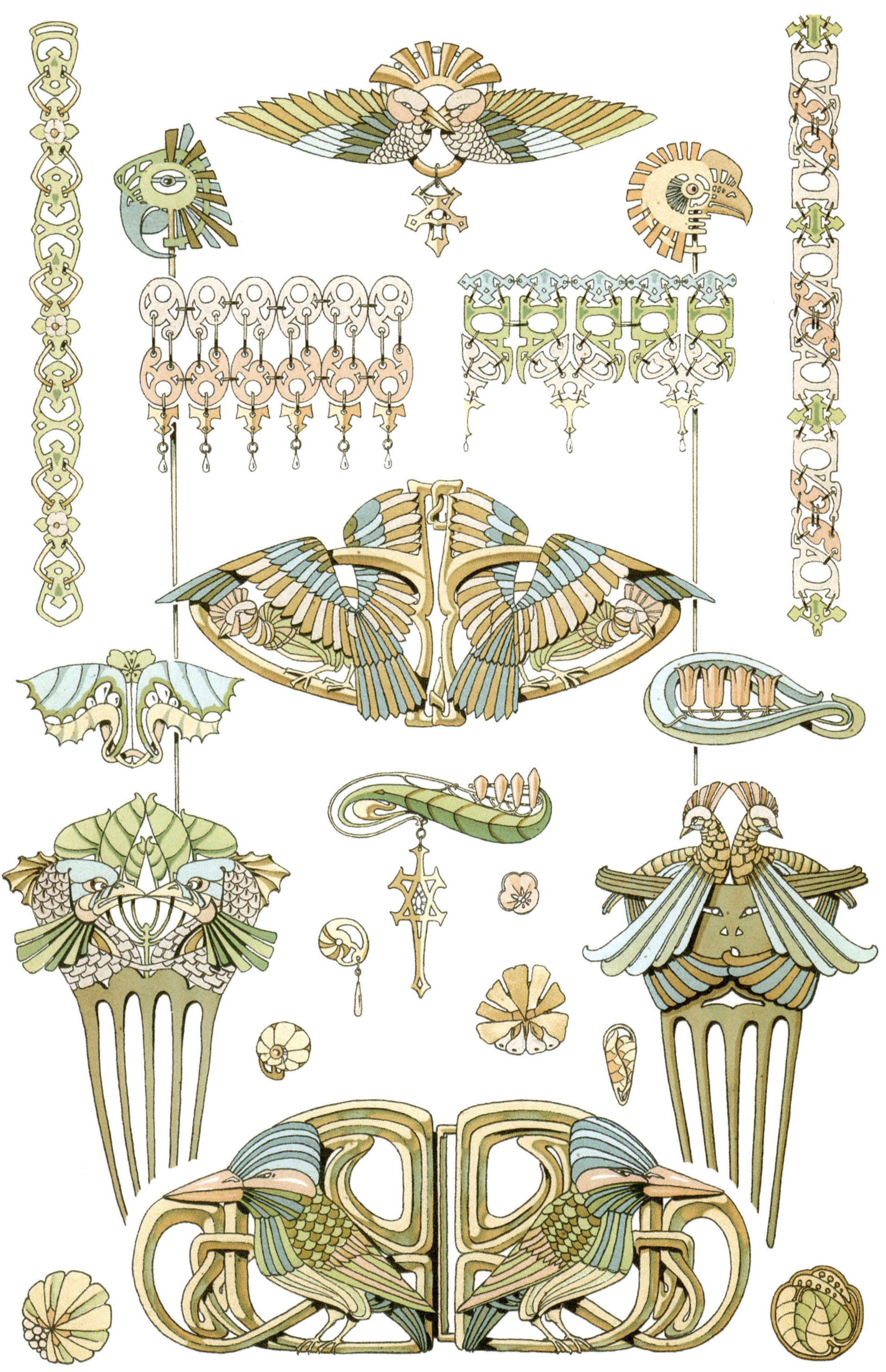

Designed by R. Beauclair

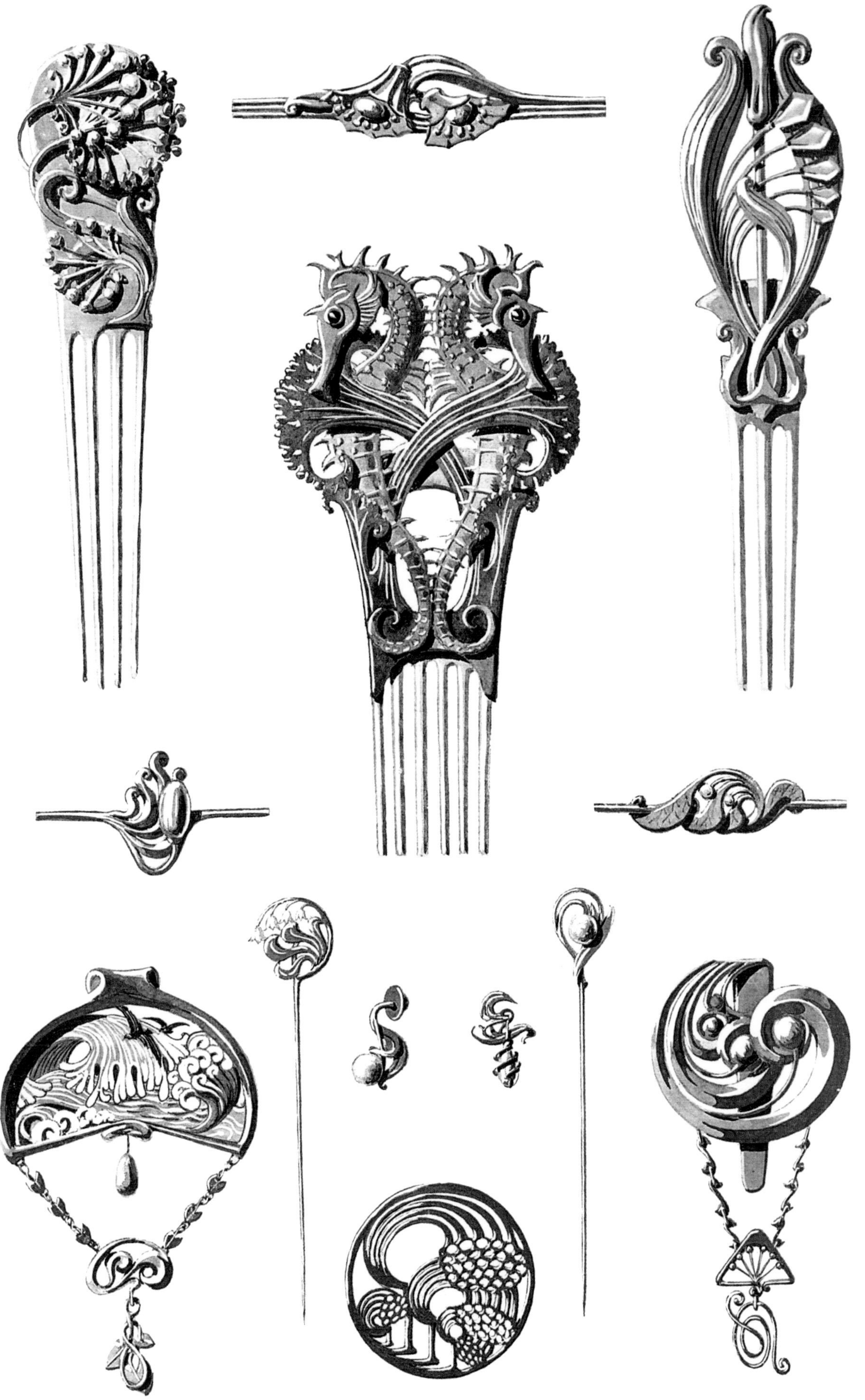

Designed by P. F. Follot

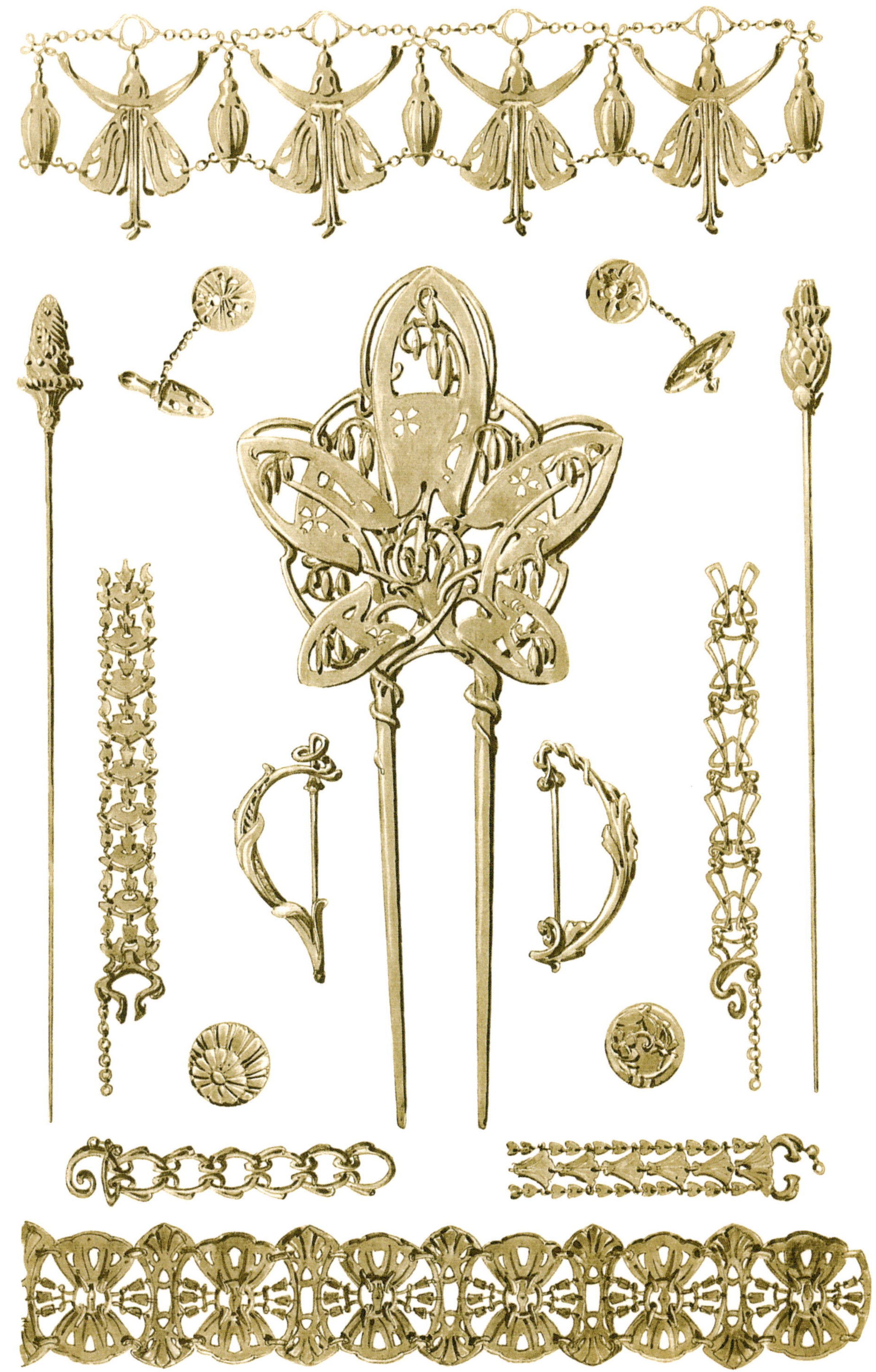

Designed by J. Armbruster

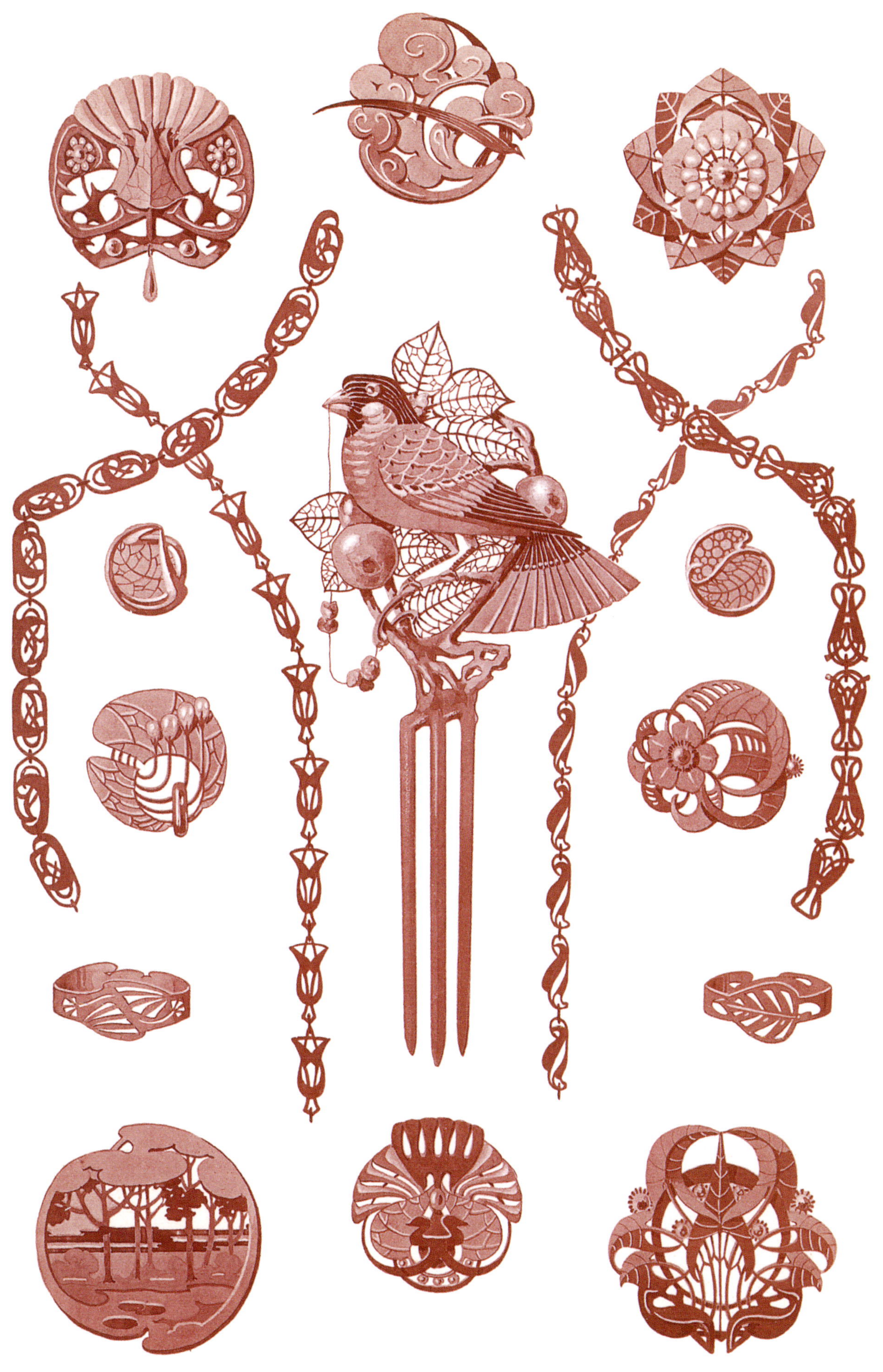

Designed by R. Beauclair

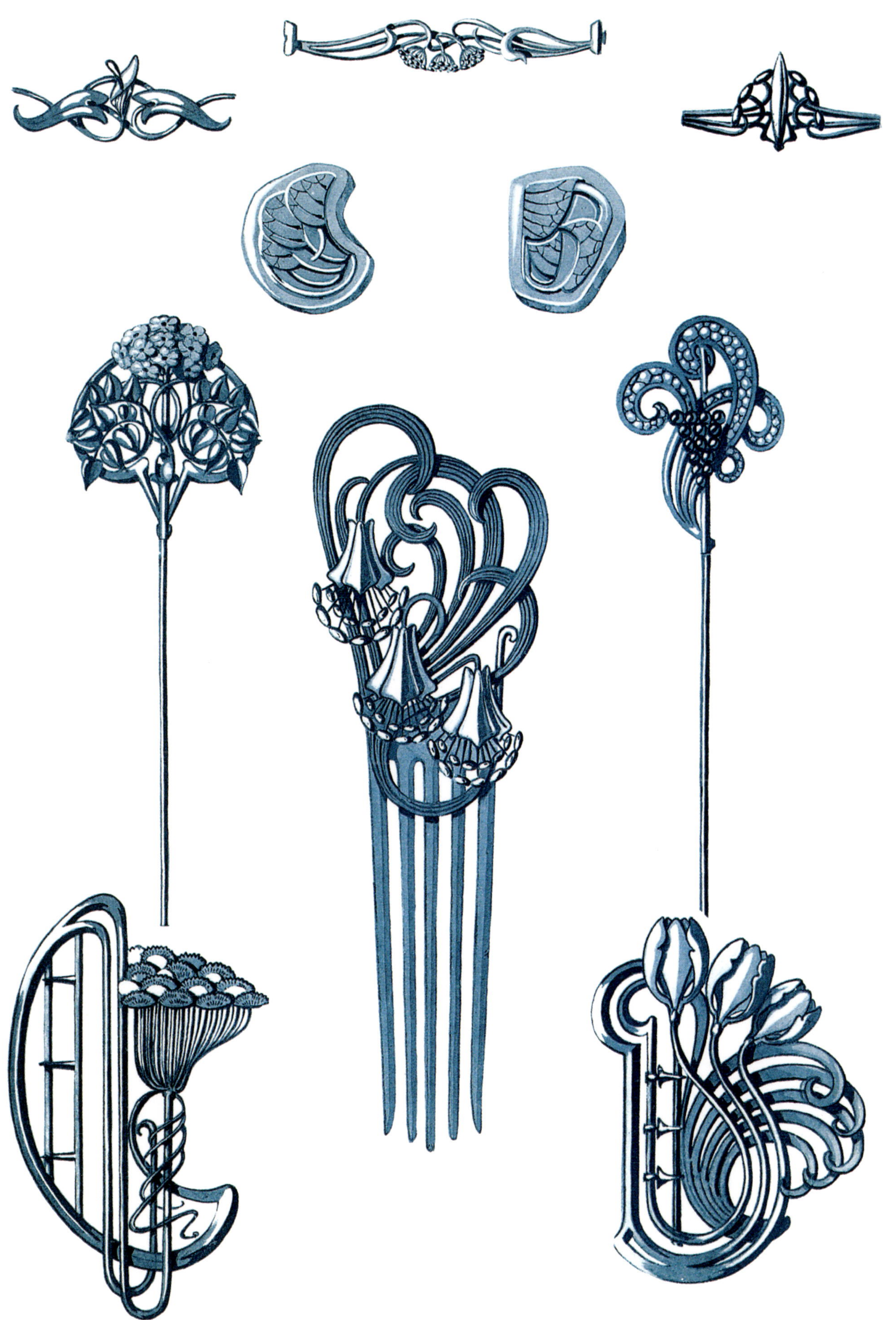

Designed by Paul Liénard

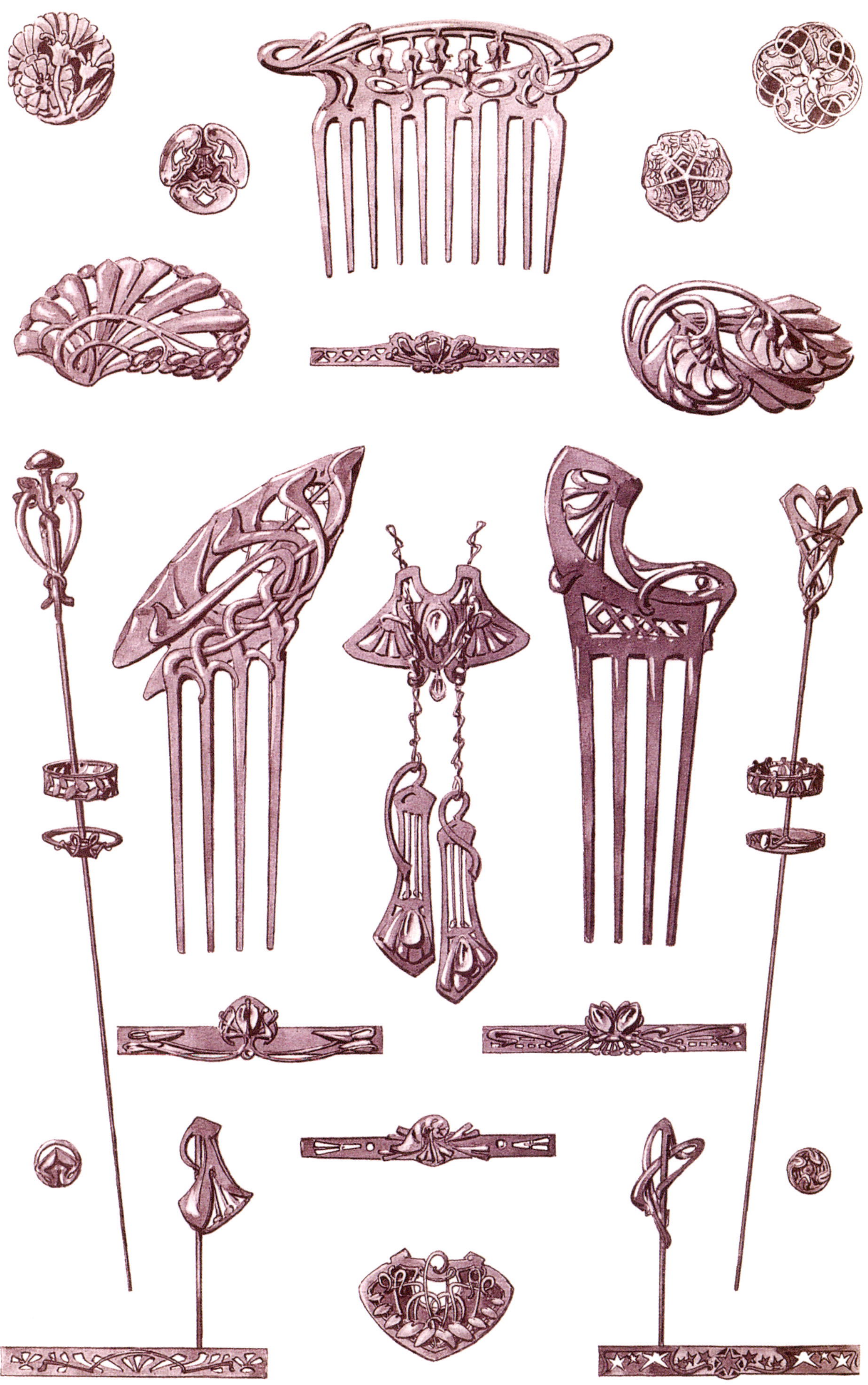

Designed by J. Armbruster